backward pilgrim

poems

by

Deborah Akers

I-BeaM
Books
2013

to my parents

backward pilgrim

table of contents

First there is a mountain.
Then there is
      no mountain.
Then there is.

—Zen saying

I already knew that mountains live and move. Long ago, when I had a child sickness and nobody could tell what it was or how to treat it, my mother put me outside in a bed with mosquito netting over it, and I lay watching mountains until they made me well. I knew that, when needed, mountains would move for me.

—Norman Maclean
"USFS 1919: The Ranger, the Cook, and a Hole in the Sky"

first things

the divine

not spark
       but flint

a stone splinter lodged
in each day's
       flammable dross

waiting for the nick
       of friction

word grit meets
       the glance of a near-
abandoned search

and the brain flares

consumes a path
       away
from its immutable source

silent forge
of every human
       firestorm

the front range

rupture, earth's tissue
ragged in high relief
is ordinary
        the day's landscape

we know the season or gauge
a storm with a glance
at granite shattered
        by sky's ice grip

heights defiant of human lungs
        a constant
peripheral sight
a comfort, even

childhood's isolation soothed
by waves of peak predicting
a future hued with
        blue benevolence

extravagant sweeps of shadow
sketch fictions
of valleys whose shelter
        deepens in storm

distant ranges imply
that a glimpse through
        the glass darkly
will please us

this torn horizon
        the true
shape of the world

solstice fruit

such a thin rind
binds our globe
of sweet acidity

a dark embrace
ripening the hidden
light's remains

then why the inevitable
tearing, fruit bared to the empty
air of hunger

all on the chance
of a random seed
            reborn

Louise

black rock embedded
in front porch concrete
first thing each summer visit
I would spit-polish and declare it
   the shiny stone

she laughed
(the only ironic
pentecostal I've ever known)
said, *The only shiny thing in this house.*

and it was true: dim brocade drapes
upholstery barely registered as
tan, maybe green,
sanitized earth tones

stern with us, her sister's
exuberant girls, she softly scolded
our mild indulgences

yet we rolled on her broad lawn
damp antidote to the dusty heat
played each worn game
left by her silent grown son

she sewed tiny garb
for our Barbies, form-fitting
red shifts blazed with white
   rick-rack

Sunday at her drab tabernacle
we squirmed, sullen
while a sweaty deacon bellowed
at dour ranchers, enduring their suits

then came the moment she turned
to us, gently excused herself, and
            sank to her knees
joined the simmer of voices
speaking in tongues

her breath became guttural
a cluttered rush of words
cobbled by the spirit

scrambled consonants clicking
            like pearls
senseless, luxuriant

each dark vowel dropping
            its small weight
into a velvet pulse

conversion

hot night under
moon-emptied sky

chalk cliffs
phosphorus incisors
seem ignited, lit from within

also ablaze, a cross-shaped
        glacial scar
scored in mountain slope
clear as a cipher

as if on cue, voices
rise from the bible camp below
easing harmony down
the valley's throat

and I am back inside
        intoxicated
by the logical gospel
of a beautiful place

back to that moonless hour
when I looked up at stars
massed in the blur of
        everything lost

said yes
to a broad-shouldered god
agreed to a sky garbed
        in orderly weave

and being so young, left
to faith the scattered gleams
of bone

straining the night

St. Elmo

for Cindi

i.

the valley's seam narrows and cinches
at St. Elmo
final mountain mining town in the Sawatch Range
abandoned
except for the lone violent woman
who runs the tourist store

sunlight snuffs out
behind the climbing car
storms start a cold boil over peaks to the north
sealing miles of sky below
as we move with shadows
up the jagged dirt road

at 10,000 feet, our lungs shrink
with familiar alarm
and we laugh at the sparse, fierce air

briefly pacing
the town's skeletal ring of false-fronts and shacks
while the surrounding green crags
darken and chill

then racing for the store's tiny porch
grabbing peanuts for warmth
the woman's eyes ice at our backs
as a blizzard of hail shatters
this high, fragile edge of summer

ii.

as the car eases between pine
and scrub oak burdened with ice
we steam the windows with stories
of other close calls

reptilian storms, as much our past
as phantom relations, brooding
above the family climate

hail clatter fades to the void
of soft rain as we reach pavement
though squalls still batter trees
in the rearview mirror

we are near forgetting
when the car swerves into
the brink of a flash flood

hillside in shreds, like stained linen
torn at the grain
bared muddy roots cling
as frigid waters dissemble
decades of soil

within minutes, granite slabs
have released the past
an embankment departs
loads of brush and gravel
dragging its wake

the damaged slope
transformed by daily ritual
of mountain storm

iii.

senses sheared
we make a slow detour
winding back down
reproachful mud roads

the sun returns, glittering on scree
and slashed trees
the way bright fragments
of dream scar
the waking mind

we rush toward relief—
dry clothes, dinner of trout
hot mineral pool
steam beseeching
an aloof congregation of stars

we've been here before:
sisters soothing ourselves
against beauty so hugely
indifferent to these foolish shelters

love, our human
hovering, the perilous
need for warmth

sunflower

noon betrays your
melancholy: grail-shaped
bloom straining its
     just-adequate
         stem

black brain
bristling with seed
     bent head
brooding the future

disconsolate

freezing fog erases
most assumptions
    of landscape

rain closes in to dowse
    the scattered flame
vermillion trees, one by one

an entire season
dismantled, while overhead
a grey-blue heron rises

    and fades, escaping
like the last remaining
shred of sky

released

sky of elm drifts
        down in small yellow
rags

travels the length
of its known
        universe

each fragment
        tracing
a labyrinth end

• • •

muttering
        beneath our feet
leaves mat into a golden paste

stem and vein
        released

theology in autumn

hesitant birches begin
the annual debate
with a soft yellow stammer

liquid ambers betray
          their uncertainty—
leaves engorged with
red veins of despair

the oaks simply withdraw
          rusting into shingles
of golden mantra

cooling air intensifies
          the argument
one by one, trees lit
like martyrs, perhaps beyond
anguish or fear

for weeks, the valley slopes
appear devoured
by every version of flame

until the last deciduous flush
          drains away
those bright beliefs
dispersed in whirls
          of small surrender

as the prevailing wisdom
gently reasserts itself:

evergreen

the divide

a simple rise
on plains to the north
      a gravitational shrug

but ten thousand feet
raises the stakes
to biblical proportions, a high

empty place—
      our secret
version of god

snow-creased ranges
scrawl harsh
      cuneiform
instructing the sky
in our hard legend:

the heavenly parent
      aloof, not
intentionally unkind

to whom falls
grave decisions
      gravity's weave wrenched

into east and west
the first freezing
moment of water

      parting ways
banished from a glacial

melting heart

fell field

for my dad

mountains are made
      by failure
even granite betrays itself
       collapsing daily

on bristled slopes
a stone spill
      casts off
from its origin

suddenly impoverished
the fell field begins again
a thousand-year journey
of boulder, gravel, scree

lichen-clenched rockface
erodes in increments

the acrid dust
      not beaten away
by sun and wind
      hunkers
in crevices
      waits
for scrappy succulents
to decay

      hoards
beads of moisture
to feed a frail humus

thumbnail's span of
      fertile soil—

either faith's
       fragile hold

or folly, burgeoning
again from the dear
       earth's heart

on mending

what remains
after the self sheds
in dry shards

when the densely figured bands
        that bind our sky
shatter:

sharp wreckage flung
        in a wide span
gradually wears
into horizon

and waiting takes
the place of weather

time-storms abrade
        the tender core
and listless moments mercifully
sheet our range of sight

until the future's faint
        blemishes
erupt once more

painful constellations
reemerging star by
        star

lost things

the heart breaks
like a calving glacier

gravity's many paths
        blaze fissures

until the ice wrenches
        free

each half bereft
yet suddenly whole

each hidden burden
        released

to the sea
        its black embrace

partial requiem

kyrie

eleison   have mercy
          upon us

elegant as granite
dense and fierce
as any good prayer

piled raggedly
then crafted
by the *kyrie*
          (christ, oh christ help

good christ)
into fallen
          slopes

need's absolute skill
revealing the heart's
          shattered landscape

sequentia

Remember, blessed Jesu,
That I am the cause of Thy pilgrimage . . .

every mountain is laden
with the remains of some
creature's catastrophe

eons of crushed lives
          crowd into
swaths of sandstone

slow red rivers vaguely
trouble the vast
          precambrian mind

with fossilized dreams
of each sparrow's fall

offertorium

heat and weight
        accumulate until

shot through with
        skeins of
mineral nerve—
the brooding ores

coal, lead
papery shale
        uranium

pocked with random
veins of epiphany
        quartz bearing gold
silver, platinum

the clear anguish
        of gems

sanctus

green-black waves
       of plainsong
ponderosa sting scent
lodgepole pine

streaked with ecstatic chords
       of aspen

all recede into a guttural
chorus of juniper and scrub oak
       at timberline

elevation tonsures
       the peak's stoic skull

enduring one more
private storm

benedictus

after rain
the front range appears
assembled in mourning

brethren
brooding beneath soaked
      blue ozone folds

oblique ancestors
informed by millennia
      (counsel spacious
in its absence)

alchemists of the base
elements of suffering
      (vanished spark
carbon ghost)
now at long-earned ease

but a beseeching eye
keen with belief
      sees this:

ancient creatures
bereft of memory, yet burdened
by mute awareness

their sheer mass unfurling
a merciful blank
on which we score
the clamor of grief

warm notes
so briefly healing

the night with
      song

lost things

            in hope
we hang
            seed bundles
outside your window

        to swing
in the blizzard's wake

birds emerge from
snowy miles

their hunger's
keen intelligence

feathering your
faded gaze

sentinel

what am I to make
of you, hummingbird
perched again
          on swaying
stem of scotch broom

at what peril
do you pause to watch
my daily passage
          by the river's grey
tongue

hunger spans your endless
          hovering
and must be met precisely

or hell to pay
          when frigid nights
erode the slim hold
of your body's flame

perhaps you are no sentinel
no courier sent at great risk
to teach the art of
          stilling instinct

but my own nature
scans the world for just
          such skills

finds haven
in these moments
jeweled with your
rapt
          attention

the Rockies at night

their black bulk
leviathan
an earth-bound sky
      bereft of stars

like a bodhisattva, or some other
      passing friend
choosing to lie down
      beside us in the dark

for this night
relinquishing even
the scattered light
      of dreams

refraction

even a desiccated moon

illuminates peaks
and sandstone
        slabs upended
by an ice age

a crowded assembly
dogged by the blackest
        night shades

frail light
        revealing
ragged features

nearly what we recognize
as haggard, the face
of an awful journey

        this is our mark
the eye's soft
curving skill—

shaping a skull
tracing a pulse in
        the alien world

trying to snow

after days of draining sky
rain draws down into a
    density

implores the plaguing cold
to wrench its
    transformation
from the icy forge

silent now night's
damp muttering

mantras dim and
    merge
into new-made hands

that spiral to their end
    with soft
        abandon

buoyed by sudden clouds
of brethren
    all ash-white

torpor

window ajar entices
        a predator breeze
winter breath exhaled from
cold-blooded membranes

it prowls the folds of
flannel and wool, keen for
        poorly furred flesh

I lie more still than sleep
forged in uneasy kinship with
the tiny vertebrate hearts
scattered through the night

that slow to near stopping
as they wait out another
        round of darkness

long hours lit by
the riddled pulse
        of a hundred hidden
                suns

the call

mother, we
        do share

a common moon
though yours is swaddled
        in storm cloud

mine barren
        with clarity's gaze

you describe a sudden spring
blizzard devouring
        your chair on the porch

while I consider luminous
pavement and cherry limbs
        clotted with bloom

chilled by the calm
in your voice, drifting
through my ear's
        helpless portal

as if already calling
from the white
        solace of snow

led to believe

shoots cannot wait
for wind to cease
      its cruelty

they stir like gooseflesh
grazed by random
      bands of sun

flung by a glum tyrant
indifferent to the riot
      roused by hope

daffodil and squill surge
      in those warm hours
until the sky is snuffed again

frigid taunts return
in force to scourge
      the tender faithful

lashed for their belief

lilacs

in bloom

aimless limbs
and bland leaves

      become bruises
on the scoured skin
of Colorado spring

cut

the blossoms quickly turn
to ruin
      scent densely blue
bountiful with shadow
marking

the edge

of winter's
hidden wound

        a dark redeemer
hallowing
the broad relentless

light

ojo caliente

steam slick rock walls
single window crusted
with years of mineral

my breath burns like the first
shock of birth

women and girls soak
then climb out, panting
on a low stone shelf

one by one, we are
called, wet and flushed
laid on narrow tables
and wrapped with flannel
then army wool

tightly: arms to sides
swaddled like infants
even the head, my brow
wimpled smooth
as a nun

set between old woman
and child
the woman smiles vaguely
then lowers into sleep
the girl whimpers at the heat
her body makes

I hover, then start
to burn
like a seed stirring
in the wet dark
or a meteor flaring
solitary, before

giving in at last
to the grip
of this planet

black-eyed susan

usually you would take on this task alone
but today I cross
the border of duty
join you squatted in the yard

the indigenous flowering weed
has bloomed the height of
struggling poplars
planted for windbreak

we pick at stiff soil
after lifting landscape stones
our trowels pry apart
myriad strands of artery root

sweating, we soon dig down a foot
and ligaments have merged
into a single green wrist

laughing uneasily, we scramble
to grip the slick, furry flesh
our hips straining as leverage

but the sinuous limb shows
no sign of giving
in fact, seems to reply
with its own
subtle greeting

daughter and mother
we have ventured as far
as we dare—

in rare unison, we
turn back the earth

help

*"I lift my eyes unto the hills
from whence cometh my help"*

generous distance blends
       blue perception
with emotion's green
to shade a dry black expanse

each day a new instruction
       in perspective—
the single gift of an
indifferent sky

though any seeker knows
we take our distress
not to mountains

but to the emptiness
clawed out by their presence

a bright abyss
wide enough for prayers to
       soar and keen

testing their span
on a merciful
       rack of wind

last things

funeral bouquet

for Lois Nance Akers

the roses barely made the trip home
buds slightly bloated
like good skin giving way

quite soon it is apparent; no use
waiting for the slow unraveling
that would replace the bloom

various small lilies hold well
with some tending (ice water run
every day over fresh-cut
stems) but characteristically eject
messy orange pollen in unison,
then fall limp as lover's remainders

after a week it is left to the workhorses
who survive their glamorous sisters
the plain ones, placed as filler

arranged with two spears of easter palm
one carnation, fragrance closed
in a soft, complicated fist

eight daisies sharing their pleasant
protestant vision—pared-down
neat white shrine

but after weeks the blooms keep staring
petals pock, begin a few
brown threads
but hold, apparently intent
on outwitting their born purpose
of propagation and pleasure

I should have known—
the bundle's endless glare,
uneasy stink of rotting stems—
where it would end

flowers in the garbage
stale water down the drain
a mottled bloom set to flatten
in my weightiest book, gently
forcing a final

release from the tough
exhausted form

backward pilgrim

once-sacred peak
too long masked by beauty
inverts most remnants
of blessing

slopes atrophy
with the dull disquiet
          that begins a quest—
no destination

pilgrims must back
          away from the shrine

though its height still
          glitters like gospel
mesmerizing, enforcing
belief with awe

only distance can reclaim
this story's true intent:

a blue
          smudge of hope
the eye's encoded
need for horizon

afterword

Wallace Stegner once asserted that an environment does not become a "place" until some artist has wrested a body of work from its raw materials. I must admit that this siren quest was the seed of this collection, set in my childhood landscape.

I was born and raised in the eastern foothills of the Colorado Rockies. In the early 20th century, my hometown was a haven for recovering TB patients. Wealthy Europeans and east coast moguls, delirious in their newfound health, built mansions, spacious parkways, and even castles back in the red rock canyons.

The Front Range was a magnetic backdrop to an otherwise conventional American childhood. A 14,000-foot mountain centered the complex of peaks and slopes that filled my western horizon. It was a daily conversation of shadow and hectic light, green and gray stone incised with snow that could arrive in any season. There was never a day that the sky did not reveal something compelling and eternal.

My hometown's latent provincialism has at times bloated into cultural chauvinism, becoming overrun with retired generals and right-wing religious groups (who viewed the spectacular vista outside their windows as God's stamp of approval). In recent years I've noticed a more disparate, desperate population roaming the streets, drawn like everyone else by the mountain's implicit beacon.

For years now I have been removed from the town, the land, the region of my birth. Yet it stays with me. These poems attempt to conjure back the fleeting sacred face that attended my childhood, to reclaim in some small way her earthly domain.